Let The Children Speak!

Voices From Students of La Salle Elementary School
South Central, Los Angeles, California

INSTRUCTOR, DR. CLAUDIA HOLMES

Jennifer Vera	Seania Johnson
Heidy Badillo	Guillermo Moran
Sophia Benitez	Jaime Lopez
Wendy Rojas	Tamera Alexander
Justin Price	Oscar Rodriguez
Kenny Price	Keila Banks
Christian Wimberly	Demani Sardin
Donaven Russell	Kylah Wells
Carlos Garcia	Ruth Reyes
Katherine Garcia	Kalani Lopez
Rachel Janee Denley	Jerell Leake
Romina Okereafor	Keidy Gomez

Published and Distributed by:
Professional Publishing House
1425 W. Manchester Ave., Suite B
Los Angeles, California 90047
www.professionalpublishinghouse.com
Drrosie@aol.com
(323) 750-3592

Cover Jay De Vance, III
ISBN: 978-0-9891960-6-2
First printing : April 2013
10 9 8 7 6 5 4 3 2 1

Dedication

This book is dedicated to our parents and teachers who love us and believe in us. We thank you Dr. Holmes for allowing us to express our feelings and thoughts. You bring out the best in students.

Why Do I Love You So La Salle?
By Dr. Claudia Holmes

Greet your angels by name: Nana, Granddaddy, Dee Dee, David, Grandma Jones, Mommy…

My Angels do, but do you know. Just why La Salle do I love you so?

Because, you are so special, so brilliant and beautiful so creative and talented, so well behaved, so helpful, so motivated and ready to learn.

You're more than even imagine at 11, 10, 9, 8, 7, 6 maybe still 5.

You are just beginning to understand all you can be when you show your best, give your best and do your best.

It seems like I have loved you forever at La Salle. It has been so many years.

You never fail to amaze me with your smiles and your hugs or when your daily effort and actions show the best of who you are. You make me happy. You make me laugh.

When they were here for me to see, my angels listened to my stories about you.

They too smiled. They too laughed. They wished you well. They understood the challenges you face. They prayed for you.

They are watching over and encouraging me to tell your story to the world. You are special. You are brilliant! You are courageous, preparing to become all you can be.

The Sky is your NO! You will determine what your limits will be. For now, you have no limits. Be visible! Be fabulous! Be the best of you.

Table of Contents

Let The Children Speak!

My Family, My Family

By Jennifer Vera

My family, my family, I love you so.

Every day I watch you and you watch me grow.

Through thick and thin we've always been the
family dad comes home to every night.

I know we go through times of strife, but then
we end up hugging each other tight.

Do you know why I love you Mariana?
Do You know why I love you Tatiana?
Do you know why I love you Danny?
Do you know why I love you Cinthia?
Do you know why I love you Dad?
Do you know why I love you Mom?

Well, that's no mystery.
I love you because you're my family.

To My Parents
By Heidy Badillo

When I grow up, I'm going to have a career.

I want the be a lawyer or something else that's BIG.

I am going to make my dream happen.

I know I am!

My parents will always be there to encourage me.

When I grow up, I am going to go to college and finish it for myself and my parents.

I'm mainly going to do it for them because they work hard and try to give me the best they can.

My mom is always telling me, "Finish school and get a career."

I tell her that I am and it's going to be for her and my dad.

My parents really care about my future.

That is why I will make them as proud of me as they make me.

These Are My Words

By Sophia Benitez

We may be mad.

We may be happy.

But most of all we should be happy

about who we are.

Who we are, not for our skin color, but for

who we are on the inside.

Each of us is like a beautiful butterfly, free to do

what it wants to do up in the sky.

Thank You

I Want to Be Like Her
By Wendy Rojas

Dr. Holmes is my teacher.

She is great!

When I grow up I want to be like her.

Dr. Martin Luther King was Dr. Holmes' hero.
She wanted to be like him.

Dr. King knew that we are all the same La Salle.
We are all expected to do our best.

This has been a special month to celebrate African-Americans like: Dr. Martin Luther King, Rosa Parks, Harriet Tubman, Frederick Douglas mad so many more important in the history of our country.

We all must get to know, respect and get along with each other, black, white, brown, yellow, it does not matter.

We must be friends.

These famous Americans made segregation disappear.

Thank You

My Mom
By Justin Price

My mom is the best in the world.

She is like a famous pearl waiting to be found.

She's always there for me. She could never be replaced.

She never gives up on me, even when I make poor
choices like show disrespect or be irresponsible.

It is not easy raising two hard headed boys alone.

When we are hungry she feeds us.

When we need clothes she's there.

She provides the roof over our heads and
the technology we have.

She loves me so much that even when I make her
angry she still gives.

I love my mom to the end of the earth.

Thank You

What I Want to do When I Grow Up
By Kenny Price

When I grow up I want to join the military and serve my country and make my family proud.

I want to come home decorated with medals of bravery and honor.

I want to join the police force and make my city of Los Angeles a safer place.

I want to marry and raise a family that loves me.

I want my children to do well in school and grow up to be somebody.

I will retire a happy man.

Mind

By Christian Wimberly

Your mind is good.

Your mind is great!

Don't ask your mom, ask your mind.

Your mind is like the center of the earth.

Your mind is a crystal in a tunnel you want.

Your mind is the moon that Armstrong stepped on.

Don't blame your mind.

Your mind is the best thing you can ever have.

Use it!   Don't abuse it!   Your mind!

The Things That Make Me Happy
By Donaven Russell

There are a lot of things that make me happy; for instance.

GOD!

He created all of the elements: water, earth, fire, wind, food, cars and human beings.

Water is an important element that we can not live without.

But that's not all!

He's done a lot more things.

We are unique human beings.

We find out many things about the universe.

We have found out how asteroids are formed and how animals thrive.

We must appreciate, respect and take care of what GOD gives.

What I'm Going to Do When I Grow Up
By Carlos Garcia

When I grow up I'm going to the military.

I will earn honor and bravery chains.

I am going to get a good education in the military.

When I grow up, I want to get married and have two children.

Who knows, I might come out dead or alive.

If alive, I will find Dr. Holmes and tell her I Achieved

Tell her thank you for making me believe in Myself.

His Dream Lives On
By Katherine Garcia

Today is a day we all sing.
In honor of Dr. Martin Luther King.

Whenever people fight to be free.
His name is remembered with dignity.

When black people weren't treated right.
He stood strong to lead the fight.

He fought with love. Not guns or darts.
He changed people's minds and hearts.

But some people didn't like his words.
He was taken away to a better world.

Yet his dream lives on that all can be free.
When we knock down the walls between you and me.

Dr. Martin Luther King's life did not last.
But his dream and spirit are free at last.

Life

By Rachel Janee Denley

Life might be tough but you make it what you make it.
I make mine rough.

The earth is nice and better than beans and rice.

God can see through you like glass in a bright light.

If people kick you out and put you down, you walk up to them
and say, "I'm back in town."

I'm tougher than you think.
I don't back down.
You don't know me!

I have the blood of a slave, but I'm not a slave.
Sometimes I'm challenged but I'm quite brave.

I'm free. I love my world and it's going to stay that way.

Ruby Bridges
By Romina Okereafor

Ruby Bridges was a young and sweet little girl
who had a heart that would never break apart.

She had faith and courage in herself that she
wouldn't
let anybody take apart.

Ruby Bridges was a hard worker who didn't let
anybody turn her life around.

She didn't let anyone mess it up for her.

Ruby was a good little girl who was not scared
of anything.

She had courage in herself and earned a good
education.

Ruby bridges grew up to believe in herself.

Rosa Parks
By Seania Johnson

Rosa Parks, Rosa Parks sitting at the front of the bus

Go Back! Go Back! With all those other blacks!

She was standing up to those policemen
saying loud and clear:

Not Fair! Not Fair!

Those white people get to sit at the front of the bus.

Rosa Parks didn't let her courage go away,
she stood up for all black people.

My Mom and Dad
By Guillermo Moran

My mom and dad are both pleasant and wonderful although they are sometimes strict.

They encourage us to keep trying when we are sad and want to give up.

They help us when they can. When something is needed for school, they buy it.

They want us to succeed in life and accomplish our goals.

They want all 3 of their children to do their best.

My sister Christina is brilliant in English and Math.
My brother Gilbert writes great poems.

I am working to be as smart as my brother and sister.
My parents will always be supportive and loving.

My Little Sister
By Jaime Lopez

My little sister may like me, but I love her.

She is my soul. She is a heart just waiting to be found.

My little sister is like a Super Star mixed with a diamond.

My little sister is smart, cool and tough.

I hope when she grows up she goes to college to get a good education.

I hope my little sister grows up and gets a good job.

My little sister's name is Jessica. She is five years old.

Triple Threat
By Tamera Alexander

I'm going to be a triple threat.
I am on my way to great success. I have no regret.

My goal is to build a wise foundation.
I'm working hard to get the best education.

I know I have to improve my reading.
I'm reading more and more every day.

Support from my family is what I need.
I'm going to get my way. I believe!

I want to go to college to craft my skills to act and sing.
Great awards and recognitions my fabulous talent will bring.

I'm going to be a triple threat watch out for my name in lights.
Achieving that dream for myself is the goal of my daily fight.

The S.W.A.T
By Oscar Rodriguez

I want to be a S.W.A.T Specialist because they
use heavy protections.

When there's a lot of gang violence, or major
crime committed,
S.W.A.T is called to get with it.

S.W.A.T stands for Special Weapons Assault
Team.

In heavily reinforced police vehicles, they carry
submachine, guns, grenades, sniper rifles and
many more   deadly weapons.

S.W.A.T uses these heavy weapons to take
down the bad guys.

As a police officer, I want to be sooo good
That I will be selected to join S.W.A.T.

That would be soooo cool.

Dr. Holmes
By Keila Banks

Roses are red.
Violets are blue.
Sugar is sweet,
And so are you.

You're like a ruby
With diamonds inside
You're the best teacher ever.
I can hardly reside.

You're careful and patient
I'm sure that it's true
And always so playful,
I've never seen you blue.

If you were a flower, I'd pick you first.

When I Grow Up
By Demani Sardin

When I Grow Up I want to become a doctor.
I want to serve our city.

I want to help our people that will need my help.

Because of my goal, I know that college and hard
work will be needed to make my dream come
true.

Working hard now is important to be accepted to
the college and medical school of my choice.

I especially need to believe in me. There will be
many challenges that I must overcome.

I want to grow up and become a doctor.

Reading is the Key to Success
By Kylah Wells

If my reading skill is the best,
I will also be the best at writing.

If I try I can be in honors classes.
For my future, I'll keep on fighting.

I plan to go to college and finish smart.
I will seek an opportunity from the very start.

Developing my skills of language will help me
believe in me.

I will achieve my dream and succeed at
whatever I want to be.

Reading is the Key to success.

I Will Be a Veterinarian
By Ruth Reyes

When I grow up, I want to be a veterinarian.

Becoming a veterinarian is my dream.

I believe I will achieve my dream.

I believe I will succeed.

I think about it all of the time.

I will begin my bright shine by becoming one of
Room 16's Absolute Magnitude Gleaming Jewel Stars

If I try hard, and believe in myself, I know I can do it.

I will be a veterinarian when I grow up.

Dr. Martin Luther King Jr.
By Briannah Riley

Dr. Martin Luther King's good works live long
after his death by violence.

Dr. King preached non-violence.

He fought without violence, but his message
was bold and loud.

He fought against prejudice, discrimination and segregation
through his speeches, boycotts and marches.

Before he died, he believed that equal rights, equal opportunity
and equal treatment would be possible for all mankind.

Things have changed, but there is still much work to do.
We are the ones whose time it is to continue Dr. King's work and
keep his dream alive.

All men are created equal.

My Dad and Mom
By Jerell Leake

My dad and mom are the best parents.

My dad and mom always feed me if I am hungry.

They give me clothes and shoes when I am in need, but especially every Christmas.

My parents are always here for me. They care about me.

They love me.

My parents buy me games to play with.

They always buy me something to ride one.

My loving parents always kiss me before I go to bed.

I love my parents.

Different Cultures
By Keidy Gomez

Black is my history and your history because it's American history.

You might say why should we care about what African Americans contributed? What was so special?

Although I am Latino, everybody's history is important. I love my history. I love Black History Month. I will always love it.

Dr. Martin Luther King, Rosa Parks, and Ruby Bridges wanted segregation to stop, to end because it was cruel to judge someone for their skin color.

Jackie Robinson and Jesse Owens were the first African Americans to play sports and be recognized for their athletic skills.

Like what Dr. Martin Luther King said, "I have a dream." and it has come true.

Well, I have a dream, it is that everyone I love is safe and your family is safe too.

I would like to give a special that you to Dr. Holmes for everything she did for this opportunity.

She is special to me and my classmates.

www.ingramcontent.com/pod-product-compliance
Lightning Source LLC
Chambersburg PA
CBHW022350040426
42449CB00006B/803